How to Install Kodi on Firestick.

The Ultimate User Guide How to Install Kodi on Amazon Fire Stick (the 2017 updated user guide, tips and tricks, home tv, digital media, streaming)

Paul Laurence

ISBN: 1544006993
ISBN-13: 978-1544006994

CONTENTS

Introduction

Tired of shuffling through the boring channels on your TV? Sick of your cable provider? To those of you who want to improve the home entertainment and cut the monthly spendings, look no further because this is your final stop. This book will reveal the magic of the software called Kodi, and the ways in which it can boost your enjoyment. All you need in order to embark on this very entertaining journey are a Fire Stick or Fire TV and this book.

The following chapters will discuss: Benefits of installing Kodi on Firestick, Details about installing Kodi on Firestick, Pitfalls to avoid, troubleshooting, enjoying the unlimited access to TV Shows, Movies and Music, and legal issues involving Kodi and piracy. We'll also take a look at hidden gems that not too many people know about. .

There aren't too many books on the market about this subject, so my intention was to give you an A-Z guide on setting up and using Kodi! It should provide insight into everything you need to know about the installation and benefits of what you can enjoy by having Kodi on your Firestick and Amazon Fire TV.

Chapter 1: Installation

In order to taste the benefits that Kodi offers, obviously, you need to have it installed on your firestick. The installation of this alluring software is somewhat involved, but nevertheless simple and straightforward. It is one of the most important things to know, and should be done sequentially. However, there is more than one way to do it, and I would be certainly doing a poor job at giving instructions if I fail to mention all of the different methods for installing Kodi on your firestick.

Below you will find five different installation methods to choose from. This step depends purely on your personal preferences. There isn't really an ideal way to do it, so whatever installation method you choose to go with, you will end up with the same result – successfully installed Kodi software on your firestick.

Method #1: Installing Kodi with a Computer and ADBlink

1. Download the latest APK Firestick files on your computer and save them on a location that you can easily access.

2. Turn the firestick on

3. Select Settings

4. Select System

5. Select Developer Options

6. Select Apps from Unknown sources; turn ON

7. Select ADB Bugging and turn on

8. A warning message will come on, Select ok. (if you know your IP address of anything on your

network, we can skip the next steps, otherwise always using the same address eliminates the need of having to look it up every time.)

9. Select Settings

10. Select System

11. Select About

12. Select Network

13. Make note of the IP address

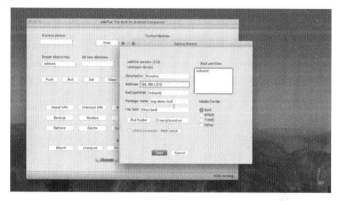

14. Download a zip file to store your Fire Stick into that can be easily accessed

15. Download adbLink for your system

16. Once installed, open it

17. Select New

18. In Description give your Fire Stick a name

19. In Address, type in the IP address you saved earlier

20. Select Save

21. Select Connect

22. See if you can see the IP address in connected devices

23. Select Install APK (This is a safe download source)

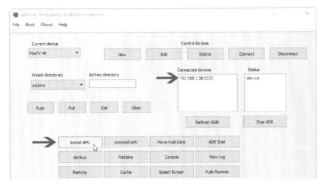

24. Navigate to Kodi APK

25. Notification will say "Would you like to install?", say "Yes."

26. You will get Installed notification when complete

27. Select OK

28. *Access through: Settings, Applications, Manage Installed Applications, Kodi, and Launch Applications.*

Link for downloading adbLink – www.jocala.com

Link for downloading Kodi – www.kodi.tv/download

Link for downloading ES Explorer – www.estrongs.com?lang=en

Method #2: Installing Kodi with Downloader – The Easiest Method

1. Select Settings on your Firestick/Fire TV

2. Select System

3. Select Developer Options

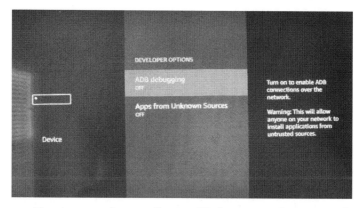

4. Turn on Apps from Unknown Sources (It is recommended that at this point you also turn on ADB debugging)

5. Go back to your home screen

6. Type 'Downloader' in the search box

7. Download and Install Downloader

8. Launch Downloader

9. A message saying "Enter the URL of the file you want to download" will appear. Make sure to enter this address: www.troypoint.com/kodistable

10. Click Next

11. Click the button for downloading and follow the installation process

12. Launch Kodi

Method #3: Installing Kodi within ES Explorer with Download Manager

1. Go to the Settings menu on your firestick or Fire TV

2. Go to System

3. Go to Developer Options

4. Make sure that Apps from Unknown Sources is turned on (again, you can turn on ADB debugging since you are there)

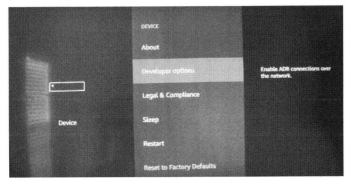

5. Go back to your home screen

6. Navigate to the search bar

7. Type 'ES Explorer' in the search box

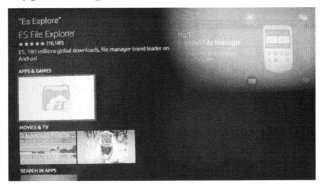

8. Click the Download button and go through the installation process

9. Launch ES Explorer

10. Into the Download Manager, input the address for downloading   Kodi www.troypoint.com/kodistable. Go ahead and rename it to KODI

11. Once downloaded, click Install and go through the installation process

12. GO back to home screen

13. Find Kodi in the application section

14. Launch Kodi

Method #4: Installing Kodi with apps2fire and a Smartphone or Tablet

1. Select Settings on your firestick or Fire TV menu

2. Select System

3. Select Developer Options

4. Turn on Apps from Unknown Sources. It is best to also turn USB Debugging on

5. Find down the About tab

6. Select Network

7. Write down the IP address of your tablet or smartphone

8. Go to the Google Play Store on your tablet or smartphone

9. Install the application called apps2fire

10. Search for Kodi in the Play Store and click Install

11. Launch apps2fire

12. Go to Setup

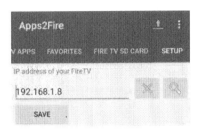

13. Insert the IP address of your smartphone or tablet

14. Go to the menu of your Firestick or Fire TV and make sure that the device is connected to the smartphone or tablet

15. Click on Local Apps from the Fire Menu

16. Find Kodi and click on it

17. Install Kodi on the device

18. When you make sure that the apps2fire has installed correctly, go back to the firestick and launch your Kodi

Method #5: Installing Kodi with ES Explorer and AppStarter

1. Go to the Fire Settings

2. Select System

3. Click on Developer Options

4. Make sure to turn on Apps from Unknown Sources. You can also turn on USB debugging while you are there, which will help you in the future. However, this step is not required for the installation of Kodi

5. Go to the Search Box in the left Menu on your Fire TV or stick

6. Type ES Explorer

7. Click on the blue folder that has ES on it.

8. Click the Download button and install ES Explorer

9. Launch ES Explorer

10. Expand the tab within the ES Explorer

11. Click on the Add button

12. Input this source: www.fireunleashed.com/as. Name it the way you want to

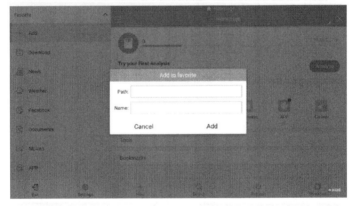

13. Click Add

14. Scroll down to the Favorites Tab and find the name under which you have saved the source from step 12. Click on it. This will open the Fire Unleashed site within the ES Explorer

15. You will see the 'Click here to install AppStarter' link. Click on Open File.

16. Install the app by clicking on the .apk file

17. Launch the AppStarter after installation

18. On the left you will see an Updates Button. Click on it

19. Find Kodi and install it.

20. Launch Kodi to make sure that it has been successfully installed

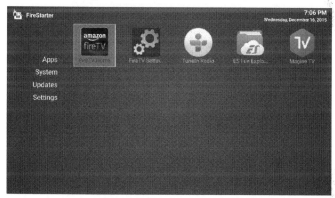

All of the methods above work for installing Kodi both on Fire TV and firestick. If you face some troubles with one installation process for some reason, I recommend choosing another method.

Chapter 2: Basic Kodi Configurations

So now that you've got your Kodi system up and running, let's spend some time talking about all of the particular ways that you can customize, configure and utilize your Kodi player to the very best of its abilities.

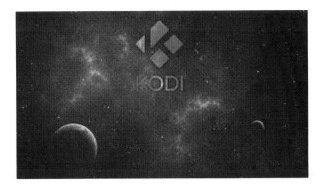

The first thing to consider when it comes to customizing Kodi is to look at the several different features available on the navigation window. When you first open up Kodi you should have the options to choose from Pictures, Video, Music, Programs and System. At the bottom is the RSS feed showing news about Kodi related updates and then you have the power and favorites button the left-hand corner. We're going to go ahead and take a look at each piece of the Kodi interface and detail how to make the best use of it.

Video

This is where you downloaded videos as well as your video applications will be there. You can stream your videos from your computer since Kodi is connected to it, so all you need to do is aim it at the folder where you keep your video media and you should be able to watch the videos that you want. Likewise, if you want to stream videos from online services, you would find them by downloading various different apps that are available to download. We'll cover apps in the next chapter.

Music

Here is where your music will be stored. Like video and pictures, you can find different streaming services that will allow you to stream music online.

Programs

This section is primarily going to be where you can download different apps that have features and functions like traditional computer programs. You can find programs ranging from Forum browsers and slideshow managers.

Appearance

The appearance section will allow for you to be able to customize the skin of Kodi as well as the language and the screen savers of the program itself. You can find different skins online to download to change the appearance, but this is an entirely cosmetic approach. Here is a list of all of the options and what they do:

Skin

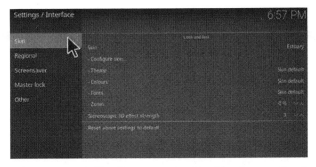

The skin is essentially how your Kodi player looks. You have the option to change the skin to another one, one that you can find online. You also have the option to change the font of Kodi and change where the home window starts up, so if you want to have your Kodi player to automatically start up and land on the TV section, then that would be the option to select. You can also disable the RSS feed here.

International

The international section is where you can decide which language to use. You can also manually set which region you are located in, what time zone to use as well as whether it is military time or if it's going to be a regular 12-hour time base. Here you can also change the formats of your date and time.

Screensaver

Kodi has a screensaver present and it will automatically work based on inactivity. Here you can set what kind of screensaver you want and how long you prefer it to have inactivity before it decides to go dim or not. You can choose between a dimmer, which you can adjust the percentage of how dim you want it to be, or you can choose to use one of the preloaded screensavers such as asteroids or some kind of wacky shapes.

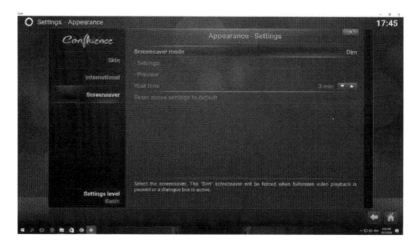

You might at, at this point, notice that there is a settings level section near the bottom of the screen. This settings level allows for you to customize how much you can change in the settings. There are four settings, basic, standard, advanced and then expert. Depending on your technical skills and abilities, you might want to consider which one would serve you best. The only thing that changes when you choose a settings level is the fact that certain settings might vanish or appear. It's nothing too complicated to worry about but if you're someone who's experienced with computers you might want to set it to advanced or expert. If you're just setting this up for someone like your parents or someone who isn't particularly computer savvy, it would be a good idea to just set it to basic so they can't mess too much up.

Library

The library section contains all of the options for how your library is sorted and grouped. Here you have a plethora of options to take, for example you can set up Kodi to download information about actors involved in the movie that you have in your library or you could group movies in sets. There are a vast number of different functionalities here, so you might want to spend some time playing around with the options until you find out what you like.

Playback

Here you can adjust the actual settings for when the movie gets into motion. For example, you can choose the original language of the stream, so that if there are multiple language options in the file, it will automatically pick the preferred one. You can also adjust whether you want it to play the next video automatically, allowing for you to keep binging on a television show. You also have the extremely powerful option to adjust how the skip button functions. This option essentially lets you choose how far ahead your player skips when you press the skip button. You can customize it to be as quick as a simple second or you can make it be up to fifteen minutes. You can also customize different intervals of the skipping rate, which means the longer you hold down the skip button, you can customize how much faster it begins to skip ahead. If you're not someone who likes the black bars in widescreen formats, then you can choose to minimize the black bars. This will cause the video to stretch out in such a way that it will try to prevent the bars from being visible.

Acceleration

If you are someone who has a souped up graphics card, then you might want to select the acceleration option and make sure that hardware acceleration is one. Most computers these days will have this functionality automatically enabled, but if you have an older machine then it won't be on.

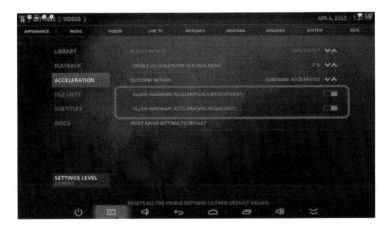

In general, this would be an area for you to completely ignore as it won't have any kind of major effect on your entertainment viewing.

Subtitles

Here is where you can adjust the settings for the subtitles. Kodi has advanced functionality allowing for it to insert subtitles into media that you own, but in order to do so you're going to need to enable it here. We'll cover how to add subtitles in to your media in the Tips and Tricks section of this book, so no need to worry about it for right now.

Discs

Here you can adjust how your Kodi player behaves when a disc becomes inserted into your computer. You can set it to play automatically when a DVD gets placed inside, and you can even choose to have it automatically try and skip straight to the menu if possible, circumventing all of the promotionals and introductions that take forever for you to get to the actual part with a movie in it.

Accessibility

Here you are able to select the default streams if there are accessibility options for those who are vision or hearing impaired. Some types of content might have special deaf subtitles, which can make it easier for those with hearing problems to understand what's going on.

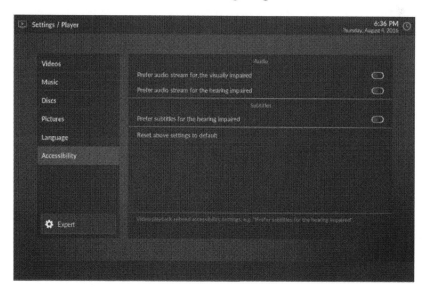

TV

Kodi does have the ability to follow live TV, depending on which kind of streams you are connecting into, so this would be the section where you are able to adjust recording options, playback settings as well as other general settings. Let's take a look at what some of the options are:

General

The general section will allow for you to enable the TV system, but in order to do this you are going to need some kind of physical hookup that will allow for your Kodi player to receive live TV, or you might need some kind of software in order to be able to emulate it. This isn't covered by this guide due to the extremely complex nature of such a procedure, but it is possible to actually turn your Kodi player into a live receiver for television. Once you do get a hookup running, you can use the rest of these options to be able to customize your TV experience.

Fire Stick doesn't have the functionality required to be able to receive an actual television broadcast, but fortunately there are plenty of add-ons that can be used to allow you to simulate a live stream but without having to receive television signals.

The music settings give you options like shuffle settings, automatically playing next tracks and how to interact with audio CDS that are placed inside of your computer. Here's a list of all of the options available to be adjusted on the music area:

File Lists

Honestly, there's nothing of note here, it's just where you can select whether you want tag reading to be enabled, which is important if you want to be able to identify the music that you are playing.

Audio CDs

Here is where you will customize whether your audio CD will automatically play when you place it in, as well as which folder your saved music will go to. Kodi has the ability to rip music from CDs, so that when you place your CD in, you can just save all of your music automatically and you won't have to worry about finding it again.

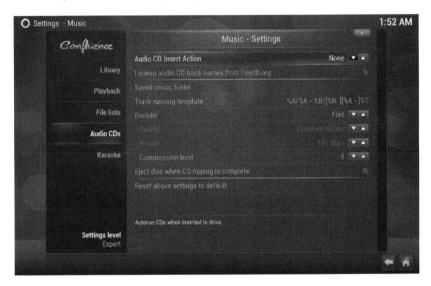

Weather

The weather option allows for you to be able to set up the option to be able to view weather local to your area. This will require a certain level of set up but it isn't too hard to do. After you set it up, you will be able to see the weather on your home screen at all times. In order to be able to set up the weather service, all you need to do is select enable weather service and then select Get More. This will bring up a menu of different weather services to choose from and then you can select which one you want to utilize. We would recommend a weather app that is local to your city as you can choose from different weather places from all over the world. Once you have the weather app downloaded, you can customize it in the settings section and choose if you want it to be visible from your home screen or not.

Add-Ons

This will take you to the Add-Ons section and we will cover how to use the add-on section in the next chapter.

Add-ons are essentially like apps that you can install to your Kodi player and it will allow you to be able to do all sorts of interesting things such as play content like Netflix or even access the news.

Services

This is the advanced user area where you can set up things like Airplay as well as remote control options. It's only recommended to use this service if you are an advanced computer user and you know what you are doing. That being said, let's take a look at all of the options that are available and go over what they do.

UPnP/DLNA

This is the section where library sharing between Kodi systems on different networks can be enabled or not. This is a relatively complicated task to do and falls outside of the purpose of this guide.

Web Server

Some users prefer to build their Kodi player to be a web server, where you can remote control into it by using an access code. This would be where you would set up the remote server access.

Remote Control

Here is where you can allow for remote control on your system. If you're using a pc it involves allowing someone to remotely access and control the player, but on the Fire Stick it isn't applicable.

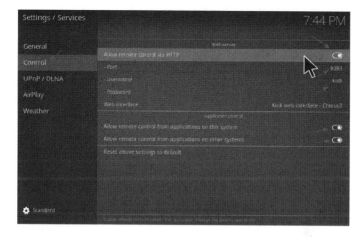

Zeroconf

This area just has one option and it isn't particularly relevant.

Airplay

If you're a user of Apple products, then you might be familiar with what's known as Apple Air Play. Air play is essentially the ability to stream video and pictures from your phone to an Apple TV. Well, with a little bit of rigging and some clever movements, you can actually set up Kodi to use Airplay as well.

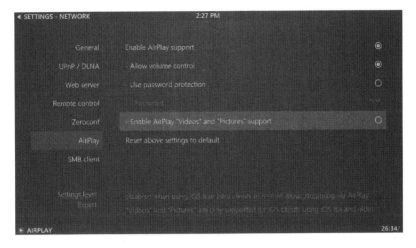

You need to have Zeroconf's single option activated and depending on what kind of system you're running, you might need additional software, but you can set it up so that your phone can access Airplay in a very limited amount. This is highly dependent on what version of iOS you are running, of course, as Apple is constantly updating their system and making it harder and harder for third parties to access their software. As of right now, it only supports Audio for anything later than iOs9, but always keep a look out, there might be fixes and hacks somewhere down the road.

Video Output

Here is where you are able to adjust the display mode, changing it from Windowed, to full screen. You can also limit the color range as well, adjusting it based on the color that your TV is able to support. You have the options to the adjust the resolution and you're going to want to find one that works best for the size of television that you have set up for a fire stick. Windowed mode will probably be the best bet for everyone else.

Audio Output

Here you are able to customize the audio channels and output device that you are using. This is great if you want to adjust your sound so that it sounds like a home theater or if you have to make some manual adjustments to the quality of your music.

Input Devices

Here you can adjust what devices you can use to control your Kodi. If you have a peripheral such as remote, it will also allow you to customize how your remote works.

Internet Access

This area isn't particularly relevant to anything that you are going to be doing, as you should already have access to the internet.

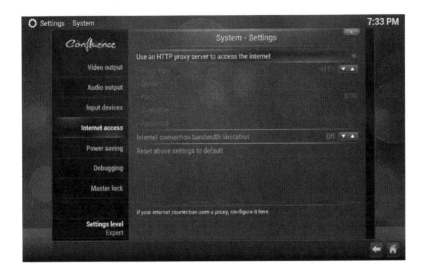

Power Saving

If you are constantly running your Kodi or someone who is forgetful enough to turn off your electronics when it's time to, you might want to consider using the automated shutdown function that times out after a certain length of time passes. This makes it a better option for keeping your power costs low and it doesn't require any kind of advanced functionality.

Logging

This section allows for you to keep track over all of the different events that occur, such as crashes, glitches, problems, etc. You can customize where screenshots of bad events go as well.

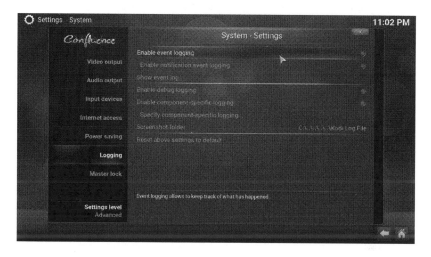

Master Lock

There are options for multiple profiles available to be used on Kodi, but the master lock gives you the supreme ability to put a big padlock on anything that you want. You could lock out the entire system at startup, requiring a password in order to be accessed, or you have the option of locking out specific areas that no one else can access without the password. This is great if you want to keep certain areas such as settings under total lockdown, while still allowing for other people to be able to access things such as video or music.

So, there is a very basic overview of the Kodi Media Center's systems and options. Now let's talk about how to get media from your computer onto your Kodi player. One of the first things that you should consider is to ask yourself how skilled you are at organization. Many of us tend to neglect organizing all of our media and have it strewn about all over our computers, hidden in certain files here, forgotten in other files there. If you are interested in getting your media act together and putting it all in one central hub, then it would be in your best interest to focus on organizing all of your media into one single area.

This practice will help when it comes to getting your media onto Kodi without a problem. The best practice is to essentially gather up all of your files, pictures, videos, etc. and put them into a series of folders marked something like "Kodi" or "Media" so that you only have one folder that you'll need to select when it comes to putting them into your media center.

Kodi relies essentially on using folders that you provide in order to be able to access your content. For example, if you go to the videos section of Kodi and select files, it will show you all of the videos that are currently available to watch. You should notice that it is entirely blank, that is because Kodi needs to be directed to the proper folder. In order to do so, all you need to do is go to videos, press files, select add video and then it will ask for you to direct it to a folder. From there you can select the appropriate folder and it will then begin to display all of the files that you have stored in that folder. The steps work the same for any other type of media that you want to use, be it pictures or music.

Once you have those principles down, it's really just a matter of loading your media player up with all of the content that you like. This is where the idea of putting all of your media into one central location on your computer comes in so handy. By having it all ready to go, all you need to do is select the folder once and then you're set for the rest of your days. It's easy, fast and customizable.

Now for those of you who are using Fire Stick, you're' going to have to be a little bit more selective with how you stream your PC media to your Kodi player due to the fact that you aren't running it off of a hard drive. You're going to need to connect through the use of a network location, which shouldn't be too hard to locate. All you need to do is make sure that you're connected to the internet and go to the select network location section where it will bring up a menu

 allowing for you to be able to add network information in so that you are able to connect your Kodi device to a shared device network. You'll need to input IP addresses and whatnot before you are able to connect to the other drives off of the PC. Once you've connected in properly, you should be able to see what's on other computers connected to the drive, including the media that they have. You can then select that media section and your Fire stick will then be available to stream information from your PC to your Kodi without an issue. Of course, this won't necessarily be as quick and flawless as if you were running it off of your PC, this is due to the fact that you're streaming the information over the network. If you have the opportunity to plug your TV into a hardline connection then it might be recommended as opposed to Wi-Fi, which doesn't stream nearly as quickly unless you have a good modem.

Now there is some work behind setting up your library past just clicking on the folder that you want to access your media from. You're going to need to make sure that you appropriately fix the settings so that your library will behave exactly how you want it to. Once you have selected the folder that you want as your target library, it will give you some options as to what the directory contains. From there you should be able to select from Music Videos, Movies or Television. Each one comes with some automatic presets that can be changed or customized as you like.

One such thing that can be customized is what's known as the scraper. The scraper is essentially the tags and information that your movies will have attached to them. The scraper automatically renames your media based on what it is. For example, if you owned a copy of the Dark Knight and had a ripped copy sitting on your hard drive, a scraper might recognize it and name it The Dark Knight and put in all of the relevant information about it for you to access. Scrapers can be set to local, so that only the information that you enter about it allowed to be accessed, or you can choose which scraper you want from a list. Official scrapers will provide more information, better titles and will allow for Kodi to be able to recognize and organize your media for you.

So, if you had a television series saved to your hard drive, a scraper would be able to recognize the episodes, put them together into a series and also put them in chronological order. This can come in extremely handy for you, as the more information Kodi has, the more organized that it can become.

So, let's talk about how the folder system works within Kodi. Kodi is an organizer, meaning that you are able to create as many different folders as you want, allowing for you to stay as organized as you like. You might have a massive collection of movies and television shows, maybe you don't want them all sitting out in one area, making it impossible for you to navigate through. Thanks to Kodi, you are given the option to be able to create as many files as you like meaning that you can effectively sort through all of the different types of content that you have.

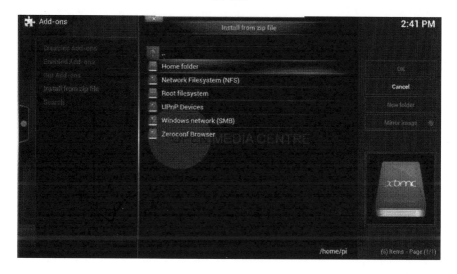

Scrapers tend to need a single folder in order to be able to effectively understand the media that you have loaded, so by keeping each piece of media in a separate folder, the sorting tags and data should be easier to discover. This is vital if you want advanced scraper functionality. Putting each television series into its own file will help with the sorting process and will keep them orderly automatically, if you try to put them all together into one big folder, it will just cause the scraper to be ineffective and you won't be able to have things like playback or recommendation applications working well for you.

Another thing to take note of when it comes to adding media, the scrapers primarily take the information off of the name of the file. So, make sure that your files are named properly so that you can have all of the proper meta-data loaded in. This will affect your ability to have things like subtitles and images to load up in the thumbnail for the Kodi player.

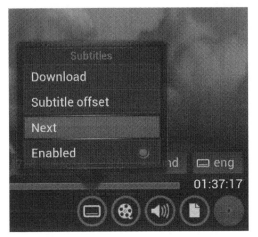

All in all, the Kodi player has plenty of advanced functionality that can be utilized if you are willing to look into the possibility of using what's known as an Add-On. These are essentially where the meat of Kodi is located. With add-ons, you can do just about anything that you want to do with your player.

Chapter 3: The Smooth Operator

Just like with any other software, the team that stands behind this amazing media center is also trying to keep up with the newest technology improvements. And while this is obviously good news for everyone who enjoys streaming content through Kodi, all of these advancements can cause Kodi users to bump into some unexpected roadblocks while playing media. These types of errors have been occurring frequently as of late because of the constantly changing upgrades not only on Kodi, but on Android, Windows, as well as other browsers.

This is surely not a reason to become 'wired' again and go back to your cable operator. In this chapter I will debunk the common problems, reveal to you why and when they happen, as well as teach you how to make your media files run smoothly again. Become the hacker in the family with these simple tricks and don't lose a minute of the incredible entertaining experience that Kodi allows.

Troubleshooting for Kodi

Before I jump to the troubleshooting issues that may arise with Kodi and show you the ways to fix them, it is of great importance that your Firestick device stay plugged where it belongs: in your TV. There is absolutely no need for your device to be unplugged when not in use, since it goes on standby by itself. It is not only completely safe to leave your firestick plugged in, but it is also recommended, since sometimes frequent plugging and unplugging can cause some problems with certain softwares, Kodi included.

It's not always Kodi's fault. Sometimes when a problem arises, it may not even be Kodi related, and it can be only a sign that your Fire device craves'refreshment'. So, I highly recommend that before taking further actions with Kodi, you cross this off the list of possible problems, and restart your firestick.

If the Kodi software is not working, and you have already restarted your firestick and made sure that that was not causing the issue, you may want to check your router. Sometimes users can be experiencing problems with Kodi simply because their firestick is losing connection to the network. Check the connection and see if that is the issue. If so, you may want to consider bringing the router closer to the firestick, removing obstacles that may block the signal, or even replacing your router.

If neither of the above solves your problem and you are still facing the same issue, then you may want to try some of the next solutions.

Below you will find the most frequent and basic troubleshooting solutions for Kodi and how to make it to run smoothly again:

Re-Installing Kodi

Sometimes, due to a number of technical reasons, Kodi can come across a glitch. If that is the case, you may want to try re-installing Kodi, as well as the add-ons. The process is fairly simple:

1. Select Settings from the Fire TV or Firestick menu
2. Go to Systems
3. Click on Applications
4. Scroll down and click on Manage Installed Applications
5. Scroll down to Kodi
6. Click Uninstall
7. Choose one of the previously mentioned installation methods
8. Go to your home screen and re-install Kodi

Buffering

If you find that your add-on is continuously buffering and nothing is downloading, you are going to want to reboot your computer. It is recommended that this is done once a week to keep it fresh.

To do this, unplug the electrical source from your modem or router, verify that there are no lights on, then wait 15

minutes to give your internet devices time to cool down. Reconnect the modem first and wait 30 seconds.

Reconnect the router next and wait 30 seconds, then open any web page to make sure you are back online. Then reboot your Kodi device and enjoy yourself!

No Volume

Sometimes when you're watching a movie, you find you keep turning the volume up, but you still can't hear it. The problem has to do with the volume amplification setting on Kodi, which just needs to be adjusted. Pause the video you are watching and click on the volume button on the lower right-hand side of the screen. Raise the volume setting to your liking. Most people generally set it at 15.0, but it is a totally individual choice. Return to your video and enjoy. The volume should be to your liking now, if not, go back and redo it.

Repository Issues

Repository Issues with Kodi that show add-ons are empty or not functioning correctly, can also be fixed easily in a few steps. First, under the systems menu, hit the settings button. Select the add-ons tab from the left side 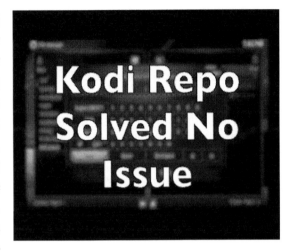 menu, then hit the get add-ons button. Highlight the repository that is giving you trouble, then click the open the context box, and check for updates. Depending on what device you are using you will need to either right click or select and hold the context menu button to open it. Reopen the repository that was giving you trouble, and now it should work fine. Repeat the process in the future if you experience it again.

Fixing Thumbnail

To fix thumbnails that are displaying incorrectly, start by selecting system, then go to file manager. Highlight the profile directory button on the left of the screen, then open the database. Open the textures13.db button then press delete, confirm yes. Return to the main menu and hit the power button, hit exit and then wait for the Kodi setup to quit. Now you have rebooted your Kodi and it should work fine.

Clearing Cache

Sometimes all you need to do is to clear the cache for your Kodi to run much faster. The tool that will help you do that is the *Maintenance tool*. The Maintenance Tool keeps your Kodi up-to-date and free of bogged down space, and ensures that it will run at its best. Like any other device, Kodi may begin to run slower over time. This tool keeps files clean and unburdened by things you don't use anymore.

This is the installation process:

Let's install Maintenance Tools first to clear (remove) cache in Kodi xbmc:

1. Go to kodi home screen go to Programs and scroll down click Get more
2. In the add-ons listed, go down and Click on Maintenance Tool
3. A new window should pop up. Click Install
4. You will have installed the Maintenance Tool Program Add-On when the *"Success"* box appears

Now, we can use Maintenance Tool Program Add-On to clear cache in Kodi:

1. From the Kodi xbmc Home Screen go to Programs. Choose Maintenance Tool(do nor forget to update Maintenance Tool from the <u>TV ADD-ONS Repository Git File,</u> you can do that by right clicking the Add-on and clicking Add-on Information and then Update)
2. As soon as you select Maintenance Tool a window will pop up "This Tool is intended for ADVANCED Users Only!", hit ok.
3. Another Community News box will appear next, hit ok again.
4. You should see the Maintenance Tool menu. Select General Maintenance

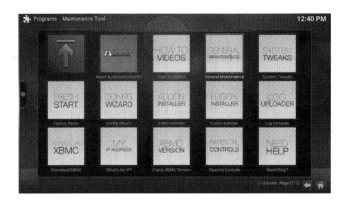

5. Choose Clear Cache

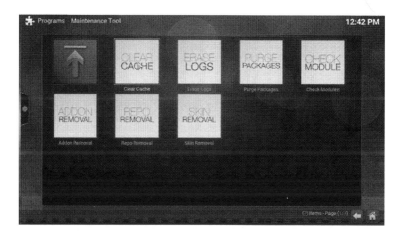

6. Click Yes to confirm

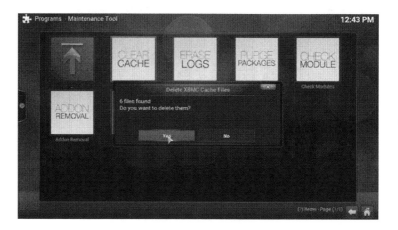

7. Then you should see "Done Clearing Cache Files"

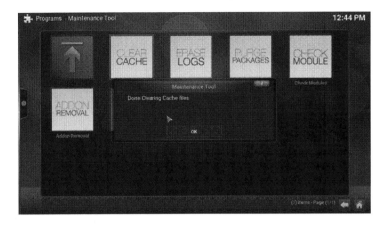

Removing Add-Ons. Sometimes a certain add-ons can be causing all the trouble. If you think that after installing one your Kodi has become much slower, you may want to consider removing it.

Here is how you do it:

1. Go to Systems
2. Click on Settings
3. Select Add-ons

4. Select the specific add-on that has been causing your Kodi to run slowly, or click on the 'All Add-ons' button if you are not sure which one you want to remove. The Video Add-ons are the most common type of add-on that will need to be removed.

Once you click uninstall, you are finished. If there are too many add-ons it may slow down your system, so it is good to remove some occasionally. You will want to do this with all your unused add-ons because left dormant, they are a perfect target for hackers to take over and enter viruses into. The viruses will most likely wipe out your entire system and allow the hackers to steal your credit card, bank account and other personal information. Try to clean them out once a month to keep your system and your personal information safe.

Posting Error Logs. If you cannot figure out what is wrong with your Kodi and you wish to get some help and support, then posting the errors you have occurred online, can help you find the right solution.

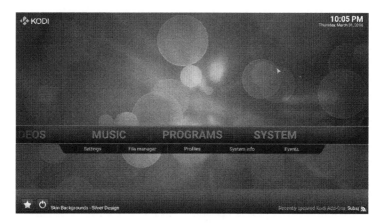

Posting Error Logs are easier than ever now due to a recent

upgrade. This allows you to upload the error log to the web so you can access it without any technical knowledge. Only upload an error log when you have produced the same error twice. If you have already uploaded TVA Log Uploader there is no need for the first four steps. If not, follow these instructions to do so.

1. Go to Programs and click on 'Get More function' at the bottom of the guide.

2. Scroll down to the TVA Log Uploader and Install the program.

3. Return to the Kodi home screen and hit the system button, then press the settings button. Another list of things will appear on the left side of your screen.

4. Hit 'System' again, scroll down to 'Logging' and then to turn on your 'Enable Debug Logging' button.

5. Now go and do whatever you did before to produce the error message.

6. Return to the main menu and hit the programs button.

7. Select the TVA Log Uploader tab, then go to the Destination Email Address tab, click that and fill in your email address press Done

8. Press Ok at the bottom of the window to save your settings.

9. Press Yes to confirm the upload of the file to the server. You will then be provided with a link on your email to connect to the forum and ask for help with your error.

10. You can go back to system → setting →system →
    logging and hit off to disable to Debug Logging
    System once again.

Updating Kodi

It can also happen for an outdated software to cause a series
of issues. It is a good idea to update Kodi frequently, and it's
as simple as going to Kodi update and downloading the latest
version. This will allow you to get the most out of your
operating system. It will run faster and cleaner when
updated.

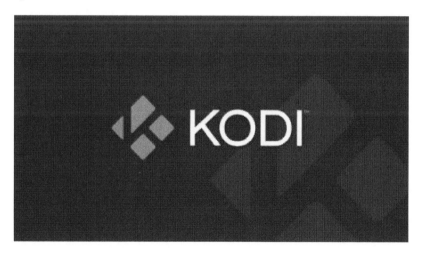

A new issue with Kodi add-ons that recently came to light in
May of 2016 is that viruses have been working their way into
a repository file. When the first questionable file was
examined it looked innocent enough on the outside. It
appeared as a popular file, but when opened the codes inside
of it completely wiped out the entire system. What else was
found after digging deeper into this breach? Let's have a
look.

Repositories are meant to be disposed of after you are done using them. Leaving them sitting there unused leaves the door wide open for hackers. The third-party sites are dangerous places to get add-ons as you really have no way of knowing what you are getting. You can compare it to downloading things on our PC, we need to be just as vigilant with Kodi and choose only files we trust.

How this works is that once you have given an author permission to run that app inside of Kodi, they have full access to the whole system. This is bad, but depending on how you are operating it could be really bad. If you are running through a system that only runs Kodi then you may have your system wiped out, and the hacker would be able to obtain information like your password and any login details you may have added. But if you are operating the add-on through your computer, the hacker would have access to ALL of your information including your email, bank account, credit card numbers and just about everything else. How to fix it? There is a Security Shield add-on you can use to detect any unused or virus-ridden add-on and gives steps to help you decide the action you want to take for such them, such as quarantining and whitelisting bad codes so they do not appear in future scans. If you hear of a developer of any site trash talking the Security Shield add-on, make sure you check the code in their add-on. The bottom line is that if it is not a secure Kodi add-on from the official repository, you are at risk.

Another tip is to <u>avoid buying fully loaded units</u>. Fully loaded units are another wide-open door for hackers to enter, but this time you left the light on for them too. These units are loaded with security flaws and make a hacker's job super easy. If you bought one of these it is recommended that you reinstall Kodi fresh  and add-on only content that you can trust. Unfortunately, there are now hundreds of units infected across the world and the users are completely unaware of the virus. Sad that these people must ruin the community like that.

Extra Support

Even though there may be nothing wrong with the way you stream media through your Kodi software, there are some tips and additional software support that every Kodi user will find useful. These next two tips can save you time and effort, and I guarantee that will be greatly appreciated by you.

Disabling Notifications. If for some reason, you no longer wish to receive notifications about updates available on Kodi, there is a way to remove them and to keep them from showing up. To start, go to the programs menu and right click the notification add-on bar. Go to the add-on setting option and click on, unsubscribe, and ok. You now have turned off your notification function. If you find you miss them, you can always go back in and turn it back on.

Restoring Kodi

There are times when the programs are too old, too slow and just need a fresh start.

When nothing seems to be working and your Kodi is way too slow for your liking, restoring Kodi to its factory configuration may be just the thing you need. Just follow these simple steps to enjoy streaming again:

1. Go to System
2. Select Settings
3. Select Add-Ons
4. Hit Install from Zip File Button
5. Choose Fusion from file list
6. Click Start here
7. Click on the plugin.video.freshstart-1.0.4.zip file
8. Return to the programs menu and
9. Hit Kodi fresh start from the add-on list.
10. Hit the Yes Button
11. Select Ok. It should say done on the screen. You will now have to reboot your device to complete the process
12. Hit the power icon and exit

13. Relaunch Kodi and reconfigure your add-on tools now. This completes the step by step instructions on whatever you need in the way of troubleshooting Kodi on your Firestick.

Chapter 4: Movies, Music and TV

Now, let's talk fun. After learning how to properly install and dodge or overcome the issues that may occur while streaming through Kodi, we have come to the most

 interesting part of this journey – the entertainment. In this chapter I will teach you all there is to know about streaming movies, TV shows or listening to music with the help of Kodi. Like I said, this 'blank slate platform' will help you access any media type you want. Think of your Kodi as the fanciest media player out there. Beats the cable, right?

Videos

To watch a video, go to the video section on Kodi's main screen and click on files. Here you can browse the videos or TV shows you have stored. It is easy to view what you have in the stored files without having to leave Kodi to do so.

If you cannot find the video file by default, there is a simple way to manually bring it up. Go to Add videos and hit browse. Find where your videos are stored and select ok. Once you make your selection, you will be asked to name it. After giving it a name, select ok. Your new source should appear in the files menu, browse for the video you want to watch, and then click on it to play it.

To stream content from the internet requires you to go to add-ons. First, click on video add-ons and then get more. You will then be given a list of default video add-ons to choose from or you can manually add a resource yourself. If you are a Kodi newbie and don't know where to start, here are some ideas that can jumpstart your enjoyable streaming experience.

Exodus

The most popular add-on for watching videos through Kodi is Exodus and it offers a variety of movies and TV Shows to choose from. There are many different versions out there, but I strongly recommend you download the newest one.

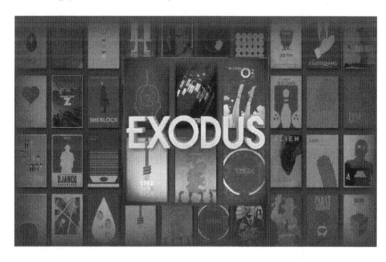

Installing Exodus:

1. In order to install Exodus, you will first need to have your Add-on Installer installed. To do so, start by opening Kodi
2. Select System
3. Click on Add-ons
4. Hit Install from zip
5. Select Fusion
6. Choose xbmc-repos

7. Select English
8. Stroll dowm to repository/Exodus
9. Wait until you see enabled notification

10. Choose Get add-ons
11. Select Exodus repo.
12. Click on Video add-ons
13. Click Exodus
14. Hit Install
15. Click Ok when installed.

Phoenix

Phoenix is another great add-on that allows streaming TV shows and movies, and it is frequently updated. From sports to children programs and shows for women, Phoenix offers entertainment for everyone.

SportsDevil

Although this is mainly a sport's add-on, many other channels can be also found on this add-on. Some of the live streams that SportsDevil offers are Cartoon Network and Fox News.

1Channel

Just like Exodus, 1Channel is a very popular add-on for streaming video, although compared to Exodus, 1Channel is somewhat poorly equipped.

There are also add-ons that only allow you to stream TV. Get one you like today, and never miss your favorite TV show ever again.

- USTV.com allows you to watch all the local channels. It is free and is a great place for service men and women to be able to stay up-to-date with their local news when stationed overseas.
- ZigZag is an IPTV add-on that brings shows from all over the world to your TV.
- Phoenix is the go to add-on for viewing live sports by going through Phoenix TV & Staael section which contains links to NFL, NHL, soccer, golf and more.
- Zeus is another great add-on for live TV and sports.
- MoneySports, this add-on links features PPV, WWE, and Live Sports.

- UFC Finest for those UFC sport fans.

If you are a fan of streaming live content, then you will absolutely love this add-on.

EarthCam -just is a camera link that you can go to watch waves in Hawaii or go see if anyone is getting married in Elvis's Chapel. You can access this through your computer as well. There are cameras set up all over the world and are viewable, some with audio, any time of day. You can look at a beautiful beach in Aruba then go to Tokyo to realize they are 13 hours ahead of us as it is dark there. This is a fun one for sure!

Music

If music is what you are looking for from your device, first click on the music icon from your home screen. You will then be given a list of three choices, playlist, files and music add-ons. Click on files. If you already downloaded music, then hit add music and browse for your music folder and hit ok. Then a prompt will come up asking if you want to add the media from that source to your library, tap yes. Then you go back to the main menu where the music is and you will be able to browse the music options by song, artist, album and year. To add more songs to your list simply click music add-ons and click get more. This way you will never get bored with your playlist.

Looking for a larger variety of music but don't know which add-on to choose? Listed here are the top five music add-ons that will make your music experience more enjoyable.

MP3 streams

This add-on allows you to download music and store it to a connected network device and lets you create a playlist. This is great if you are having a party. It offers all the latest albums to choose from as well.

Installing Mp3 Streams:

Kodi 17 Krypton download.

1. Go to HOME Screen

2. Go to Add-ons and sekect Settings button

3. Enable Unknown Sources.

4. BACK to HOME screen and choose Settings button. Click on File Manager and Add Source.

5. Enter http://fusion.tvaddons.ag in the top box and Enter FUSION in the bottom box. Hit OK.

6. Go back to HOME screen. Select Add-Ons and Add-on Browser

7. Install from zip file. Click on FUSION and then on kodi-repos. Choose english and type repository.xbmchub-x.x.x.zip.
8. Wait for Add-on enabled notification.
9. Install from repository. Next select TVaddons.ag addon repository. Hit Music add-ons and select MP3 Stream. Click on Install.
10. Wait for Add-on enabled notification.
11. MP3 Streams is now installed and ready to use.
12. The Add-on can now be opened from HOME screen.
13. Go to Add-Ons and select MP3 Streams.

Music Box

You will need to create an account with VK.com; this will give you access to music through links like Digster and 8Tracks. Music box also gives you access to movie soundtracks if you like that sort of thing.

Rave player

This one is great for more old school music, and has a section of a DJ Mix sets to choose from. It also has live Radio stations, video radio stations, and Podcasts available. There are garage bands, house bands and jungle sets with this add-on too.

Jango.

Jangro gives you music from the Jango.com database. It gives you hundreds of music choices including genres, feelings and seasons. You can create stations to include specific artists and songs, and have the option to play music videos from that song. Unlike the other add-ons which stream music through YouTube and other sites, Jango streams it through the web, which allows you to quickly and clearly hear the music you desire. After registering there is an option to add your phone to the service allowing you to play music free from your phone.

Music Source

This add-on is said to have something for everyone and includes a music trivia section to test your music knowledge. This source has the best live music choices, old school music, DJ selections and videos around.

You must know that streams come and go, so what worked yesterday may not be available today, so the above sites may be obsolete already. For example, Genesis is now replaced with Exodus. So, if you are trying to run Genesis and find it completely abandoned, it's because it is! The developer is now operating Exodus. If you search around and explore inside the world of add-ons through the safety of Kodi, you may be surprised at what you find. Go and check it out!

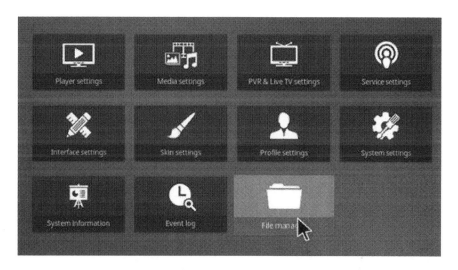

Using Kodi's website and forum is another good way to stay on top of the latest news, topics and downloads they have to offer. The forum is a good way to communicate with the company as well as other users. They offer tips on how to install and uninstall add-ons. There are step-by-step guides as well as tutorials to assist you with various topics. There are how-to guides which provide answers to all your questions. They keep you up-to-date on the latest video, TV, and movies that are available. They also offer giveaways to people who register and play.

The Safety of Streaming

Many people question the safety of the Kodi software, mostly because it is an open-source that is completely free. Because Kodi operates by utilizing an open forum with add-ons that can be shared with the community, there is a strong potential for viruses to enter your system undetected. To protect yourself from these viruses, you should have a VPN or Virtual Private Network. The VPN protects your identity by encrypting your connection so that no one, not even your VPN provider can monitor what you are watching. Most of the VPN services cost around $5.00 a month. Free VPN providers are usually overloaded and sluggish, giving you slower download time. Free VPN providers also get their money by selling ads as well as selling your browsing history. That means your privacy is in jeopardy. One of the best VPN providers is NordVPN. It is easy and quick to install. This service also allows you to unblock Kodi add-ons so you can add-on anything in the way of streaming movies or TV channels you desire. Another is Pure VPN, which sometimes has specials starting at $2.45 a month for 2 years. Another great VPN is called Hide My Ass, it is available in 190 countries. The software is straightforward and easy to use. It is recommended that you purchase a VPN from the country you're streaming from, such as from a U.S. server if you live in the United States.

So you know, there's a difference between virus protection and a VPN. Virus protection is a program that looks for, detects, removes and prevents viruses like malware, adware, worms and Trojans. They do this by scanning files to detect any known malicious patterns. You can manually schedule these scans as often you like, and your computer does the rest. Virus protection also allows you to scan specific files and will remove any infected files. Some programs warn you about the dangers, while others simply do their job quietly. Updates will then be given to you by your computer after a scan has happened letting you know what it found. Virus protection is recommended and is definitely worth the money.

VPN works by using the internet or public wires and connects to a company's internal network. There are many ways to use networks to transport data, with networks encrypting their system to ensure that the messages are not interrupted. It is a protection in the sense that hackers cannot see anything from your computer because there is no direct connection between your computer and the hacker's device, but as said there is the potential to upload an add-on that is infected since they are not monitored and approved by Kodi. Uploading bootleg or pirated movies still have the potential to contain to give you viruses.

There is also something called Proxy. Proxy allows security only to your torrent client or web browser. It does not protect you from 100% of all your internet access. With a fully anonymous VPN all your information is secured, so choose a VPN over a Proxy.

Chapter 5: Hidden Gems

There are many different ways in which you can squeeze the most out of your Kodi and enjoy unlimited content through this award-winning media center. From the web interface that will help you achieve that, to teaching you the ultimate hacks that will make you a real king of entertainment, this chapter reveals to you the gems hidden inside the land of Kodi.

Web Interface

Web interface is what allows the users to interact with their Kodi through a browser. The users do this so they can manage their media libraries, for a remote control, or many other extremely useful things.

Chorus 2

The newest, most popular and safe to say, the best web interface for Kodi so far, is Chorus2. Kodi has a web interface which allows you to browse and playback directly from your Kodi device. It is a service which Kodi never really promoted and they don't really know why. Over the years, it wasn't used much, and there were so few upgrades that it fell by the wayside. That was until a web developer showed up on the Kodi forum saying that he had been working on Chorus for some time. The people from Kodi liked the look of the new web interface design and asked this developer to join the team, and fortunately, he agreed. He began working on a new interface and called it Chorus2. The new version was much nicer, so folks at Kodi decided to skip version 1 and went stuck with this newer and better version 2.

We will look at the potential of this new interface. First, it has a fresh new look with a modern flat design. It adapts to different size screens but works better on larger screens. It is easy to add new languages and can have many languages within it. You can customize settings and menu items. You can enable and disable Kodi add-ons easily. You can configure application settings for headless set-up with Kodi. There is a help section that enables people to make their system run better. By using a browser, it gives the user the ability to file an add-on media that is not in the Kodi library. It comes with a remote control to navigate through Kodi UI and controls volume, playback, progress and repeat. There is Kodi keyboard control. You can send text to Kodi. The new interface can trigger scanning of audio and video libraries. It will also take a screenshot of Kodi and has support when it is needed.

The Playlists add super easy to Kodi audio as well. You can create and manage playlists that store in browser local storage and in Kodi playing queue. You can filter, sort, and search using artists, movies, albums and TV shows.

You can view information like a movie description, the cast, directors, the year and the AV quality. You can get movie set information, watch trailers, stream video and download video from your browser.

For audio, you can view artists, album pages, genre, and mood information. You can look up music videos by using the song, and you can play them in the browser of Kodi if YouTube add-on is installed. You can import saved playlists and create local streaming too.

The most important thing we can mention here is how to get it working. Start by going to Kodi Settings → service settings → control. Next allow remote control via HTTP, and allow remote control from applications on other systems. Click the Web Interface button and select Kodi web interface-Chorus2. Change the username and then the password. It is recommended that you do not leave this empty. Note that the port number is 8080 by default. To access from the same computer, use this address: Open http://localhost:8080 in a web browser. To access from another computer: Get the IP address for the device running Kodi by going to Kodi settings, system information and note the IP address and open http://your-ip-address:8080 in a web browser.

Arch

Although compared to Chorus2, the add-on Arch may not seem like that precious of a gem. However, this web interface has proven to be super useful, so I believe it is indeed worth mentioning. This modern web interface allows you to access your favorite media, as well as discover new content directly from your laptop, tablet or phone. If you want to give it a try and see if Arch can satisfy your entertaining needs, here is how you can install it:

1. Go to Settings
2. Select Add-ons
3. Hit Install from Repository
4. Hit Get Add-ons
5. Click on Kodi Add-On Repository
6. Select Web-Interface
7. Find and select Arch
8. Click Install

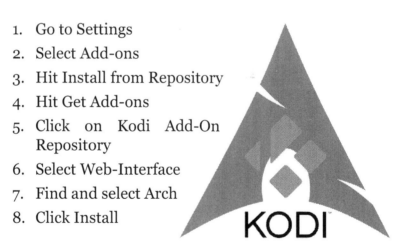

The best part about those web interfaces is that you can actually use more than one of them at once. To do so, you will need to know the IP address from which you access your add-on for the default web interface. Then, by simply adding /addons/ to your IP address (for instance http://5568.5.8.9:8080/addons/) you can see a directory listing.

Chapter 6: Tips, Tricks and Hacks

Want to improve your Kodi experience? These next tweaks will make you a real streaming master.

Change the Look

Skins on Kodi are the appearance you see on the screen, like colors and menu options, and can be changed easily by the user. They are a matter of personal preference and are available through Kodi's menu. Aeon Nox is one of the most used skins. It is easy to negotiate around the screen and is simple to use. There are a lot of options with this skin and people seem to like this one. Amber is another user-friendly skin, but it is recommended for use on less powerful devices like the Raspberry Pi. This one also offers some customization so you can make it to your liking. Bello is another skin to use on less powerful devices. It is simple to use and super-fast. The default skin for Kodi users is the Confluence.

It is simple and easy to use, but still offers room for customization. Many Kodi users never venture away from this skin because of its great features. Eminence allows more content on your home screen. You can add playlists and all kinds of things, which makes finding what you are looking for very simple. Refocus is the most popular, down-to-earth skin, in that it works on lightweight devices and it works well. The last skin is called Mimic. It combines the Aeon Nox and the Refocus to make it a middle of the road skin. It takes the customizable Aeon Nox and the lightness of the Refocus and blends them together to give you the best of both worlds. Choosing a skin is a very personal decision, you need to take into consideration the device you are using it on and what options you like best. You don't want a super customizable skin on your lightweight device that will bog it down. However, you could enjoy choose one for your heavier duty devices because you like having all the content right up there on your screen. Again, it is a very personal choice and the ones discussed here look to be a cut above the rest.

Save Yourself the Trouble

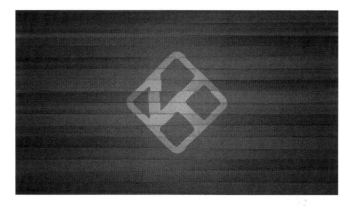

Other hidden tricks up Kodi's sleeve are built in as backup. If you hate doing everything step-by-step you will find these next time-saving hacks to be extremely useful.

- The first is that by holding Select and Play for 10 seconds, you will initiate Fire TV to restart.

- Next, by holding Right and Back for 10 seconds it will prompt you to reset your Fire Stick to factory reset. These little tricks were put in place in case there was no way to access your Fire TV's menu.

- To cycle through various resolution settings, hold the Back-Reverse-Right-Select simultaneously for 10 seconds. It will scroll through the selection once every 10 seconds until Select is pushed. This setting was developed to work in a case where your TV does not support Fire TV's resolution. Funny thing is that when you use these options you can choose 480p though it is not available in the resolution options of the settings menu. But at the same time, it appears to be continuously rendering at a resolution of 1920 by 1080, and it does not matter what the resolution is set at under resolution options. This shows up when a screenshot is taken.

Manipulate Your Media

The Context menu is an advanced menu that allows you to manipulate files and open extended option files. The device you are downloading it onto will determine the method to use for downloading this function. But it is recommended you download this function in any case to enable you to view movie and show information when a movie or show is highlighted.

Increased Privacy

One last hidden gem with Kodi is that it gives you the ability
to keep your source more private. You will use lock codes and
passwords to protect that source. This can be accomplished
by going to settings, system and master lock. After enabling
the master lock, a set lock button will pop up in the context
menu which will allow you to lock a specific source. You will
need to create and remember the master lock code and
create a password as well. That source is now only protected
in Kodi. Outside of Kodi your source is not protected in any
way.

Conclusion

Thank for making it through to the end of How to Install Kodi on Firestick: Complete User Guide to Installing Kodi on Your Firestick and Amazon Fire TV.

This book covered quite a bit in the way of Installing Kodi and its myriad benefits.

We explored how you can enjoy TV shows, Movies, and Music using Kodi on your Firestick and Amazon Fire TV as well.

But, please, be aware that the author of this book is in no way associated with Kodi and that any recommendations are based on a research.

Finally, if you found this book useful in any way, a review on Amazon is always appreciated!

Thank you for reading. I hope you enjoy it. I ask you to leave
your honest feedback.

I think next books will also be interesting for you:

Amazon Echo: Dot

Amazon Echo

Amazon Fire TV